DOGS
(and other funny furries)

*Written by children
for pet lovers everywhere
Edited by
Richard & Helen Exley*

*Published by
Exley Publications
(in the United Kingdom)
and Angus & Robertson
Publishers
(in Australia)*

To Mum and faithful old Gyp.

By the same editors:
The Missionary Myth (1973)
Grandmas and Grandpas (1975)
To Dad (1976)
To Mum (1976)
What is a Husband? (1977)
Happy Families (1977)
Dear World (1978)
Cats (and other crazy cuddlies) (1978)

First pulished 1978. Copyright © Exley Publications Ltd,
63 Kingsfield Road, Watford, Herts, United Kingdom, WD1 4PP.
Second printing August 1979
ISBN 0 905521 21 8 (UK)

Published simultaneously in Austrialia by Angus & Robertson Publishers.
National Library of Australia card number and ISBN 207 13750 1

Front cover drawing by Gail Agrisanti, 7
Title page drawing by Alexandra Slater, 7
Back cover drawing by James Peasnell

Printed in Great Britain by Morrison & Gibb Ltd, Edinburgh.

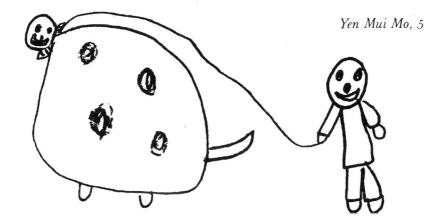

Yen Mui Mo, 5

Introduction

Our thanks go to the thousands of children who sent in entries for *DOGS and other funny furries,* and to the many teachers and friends who helped gather them all together. We are only sorry that the book couldn't be twice or three times as fat because the only unenjoyable part of the whole project was having to say no to so many thoughtful, creative or funny entries. Apart from that one sad job, the book, and its companion, *(CATS and other crazy cuddlies),* have given us days and months of fun, making our work positively entertaining.

No entry has been invented or embellished. We've even left the sometimes atrocious spelling. We sometimes chose brief extracts from long essays, but all the drawings and words are the genuine unaltered work of the children.

Richard & Helen Exley

3

What is a dog?

Pets are a part of our lives.
What would we do without them?
After all, rugs, slippers, knitting
   and fluffy toys, would all be unchewed.
We would leave things around,
Without worry or care.
Wouldn't life just be a bore
When nothing is a mess?

Joanne Woodward, 14

My dog means a long, pink licking tongue on my face to wake
me up. My dog means mother's unbreakable dishes broken.

Andrea Nicholls, 11

A dog doesn't bear a grudge.

Robert Simpson, 11

Andrew Ravenscroft, 9

4

Dogs lay down as quiet as a falling hair. They snuggle down upon the best chair.

Stephen Aindow, 12

A police dog is really a policeman with four legs.

Robin Connor

A dog is an animal with big friendly eyes.
A dog barks for joy but whines in sorrow.
A dog buries bones in his masters vegetable patch.
A dog pinches the best chair by the fire.
A dog barks and yelps in his sleep.
A dog is a life-long friend.

Catherine Smith, 13

A guide dog is a blind persons eyes.

Mandy Simpson, 11

Dogs understand but cannot tell anyone.

Karen Howard, 13

A pet is a paw on your knee at walk time.

Jennifer Jackson, 9

A pet means chewed slippers, missing hairbrushes and threadbare carpets.

Debbie McNamara

A dog's best friend is a man.

Nigel Dunn, 14

A dog will always lie by the fire to stop you from getting too hot.

Robert Simpson, 11

Life with a dog

A pet is under the chair when the vase has been broken.

Michael Lawrence, 10

A pet is a puddle on the kitchen floor.

Jennifer Jackson, 9

A dog is something that has to be taken for walks on Sunday when Dad wants to read the paper.

Mark Harvey, 9

A dog is a giant hairbrush.

Timothy Atkinson, 13

Dafydd Brynmor Evans, 13

A dog is something to drag you off your feet in the park.

Annmarie Howard

My cousin goas mad with the dog somtimes she *kisses* it.

K Pern, 9

Robbies fur is rough and dirty and his feet are smell very cheesy. These are some nick names for Robbie our dog. Scruff, Hoover, Dustbin, and Scruff Carpet.

Christine Drake, 11

My dogs name iss Taffy
When he barks you get a fright
And if your a burgular he'll give you a fight.
The neighbours get up and shout,
'Be quite you little _____

Leslie Black

A dog is for eating dad's cap.
A dog is for chasing cats!
A dog is for tying you round a post.

Tim Haslam, 12   *Mathew Prosser, 13*

When I was one year, two months and five days old, my brother
was born. When my brother came back from the hospital, my
dog could not take the strain of both of us, so he ran away.

Peter Potts, 11

I like to copy my dog but I do not like chewing shoes.

Ruth King, 10

My pet is called Princes. He is a boy. He manliy lives in the TV
room between the chairs.

Paul Casson, 8

It's always easy to tell that our dog Bruce has been in a playful
mood by my bleeding hand.

James McDonald, 11

My dog chewed my big
brother's digital watch and
he got a row. My mum said
he was to get put down. We
said we would go with him.

Jennifer Hoskin, 8

I have a dog called Lassie
She loves to eat her bones
She's like Shirley Bassey
Your ought to hear her moans.

Michael Plummer, 8

Jackie Potton

7

Dogs!

We had Rebel for five and a half years.
When she was one she had 6 puppies.
When she was two she had 6 puppies.
When she was four she had 6 puppies.
When she was five she had 7 puppies.
Rebel has always been a feckless dog.

Julie Duggan

My dog has a habit of nipping any four legged animal it sees.
That is why we keep him on a lead every time we go see Auntie
June and her seven month old baby.

Emile Crossley, 11

David Angell, 7

We had some freinds once and they had a dog called max and whenever it saw something danglind it jumed up at it and bit it. So you can imagne what trouble I had with my school tie.

Nicholas Pattinson, 9

Being so young, the puppies obviously missed their mother, so my father gave them a home-made draught excluder as a compromise.

Rhian Rowlands, 14

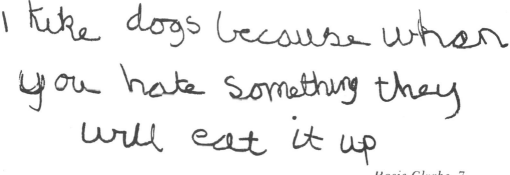

I kike dogs because when you hate something they will eat it up

Rosie Clarke, 7

Demolition experts

My mum can not wait to have a dog why? because Dad weres his old clothes to mass. Mum wants to the dog to bite dads old clothes.

Marc Wiehe, 7

Our dog riped up all our capets and rugs and it riped up our slipers. and we sold our dog to my cousin Peter.

Alan Troy, 8

A pet is your friend for ever... until he chews your new slippers.

Joanne Woodward, 14

I have got a labrodor. His name is Lucky. He chews my dads slippers up, he likes the sole of the slipper. He loves his big fat jucy bone. He likes to eat my dolls hair. When my little brother isin't looking he takes his cars and lorries and chews them up. When my mum goes to her bed she lies her nylon dressing gown in the kitchen and the dog chews it, There is a big hole in it. When he goes to his bed at night he tears the wallpaper and pulls his blankets out of his bed.

Denise Kilpatrick, 8

I have a dog I liked him but he had horrible hubbits for instance he ate my clothes and he ran away under the wire and we had to go looking for him and one day he ate a pare of my sisters tightes and when he woke up in the morning they had come out the other end.
Every night instead of sleeping in his basket he went to the porch door for two reasons, one to be on guard and two he always ate the wallpaper, my sister named him tarzan because her name is Jane.

Richard Levy, 7

We called our puppy Mistter Spock. Spock ate my sister shoses. Spock got a beting. Spock made hols in my pyjamas. I had three pairs of pyjamas. My third parir of pyjamas is one sleeve ton off. My first pair of pyjamas have holes efreewair and my senked pare iswell.

Jeffrey E Wood, 8

Floss our dog is the best demolistion dog we have ever had.
Helen Maccallum, 10

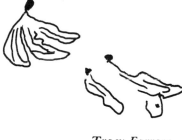

Tracy Farrow

11

Who's daft then?

Rusty has a dreadful habit of going into our rooms and taking cuddly toys. He then takes them into the sitting room and beats them up, shaking them from side to side. If you take the toy away from him, he then does a 'Mad Harry Act'. He tucks his tail between his hind legs and runs round the house at top speed.

Ingrid Sawers, 11

We have got a dog called Tickar. When Tickar gos to get the cows in she swings on the cows tails.

Stephen Allan, 9

I would like a Dog which wouldn't keep looking in the mirror!
Tristram Compton, 9

Michael Craig, 9

Our dog is a nusiance sometimes. But at other times you can dress her up in dolls clothes and put her in a pram and she stays there untill she sees a cat when she jumps out dolls clothes and all. We try to stop her but we can't.

Clare Waterworth, 8

I sit Buggins on a chair beside me and we share my tea. She has been in doll's clothes and in a pram, in my bicycle and on skates.

Alannah Moore, 8

My friend Trigger the Alsation,
He is very big and has a bionic kick,
And a very big bushy tail.
Trigger the Alsation was scared out of his wits,
By My little Hamster who is very cuddy and very soft.

Robert Mills, 11

My dog Goggis is as daft as anything. I don't know if he'd make a good guard dog he'd either bark his head off lick the burgalar to death or hold his torch for him.

Amanda Wren, 10

I have a dog called Nutty. We got him from a friend when he was called Noddy but we changed that to a much more suitable name.

He only does two tricks and even they are a bit nutty, that's why he does them. The first one he learnt was to take his tail to bed. You tell him to catch his tail and then with it still in his mouth he walks to his bed or up-stairs. The second one he learnt was with a piece of cake or food. You say 'Its mine' and when you say, 'Good boy' he flicks it up in the air and then eats it. When we first got him he found a dead rabbit. We found it after wondering where the smell had come from! When some one lets him out into the yard Mum says he's gone to exercise his voice.

Dorothy Young, 11

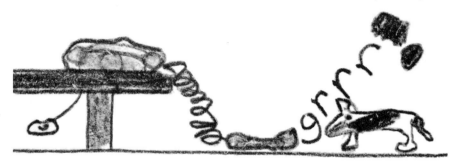

My super pet is a spaniel. Every time he hears the phone he is down like a flash. He attacks it as if it where his bone.

Michael Pern, 12

Homer was a black and white dalamation. Homer was a brillant footballer. He was a brillant goaly also. He used to go in goal for my side. Homer most times burst the balls though.

Jeremy Nickalls, 11

My dog allways plays Rugby when I wont to play football.

Thomas McClimonds, 10

I brought a dog who ran round and round after his tail. He could never catch it till he lay down.

Robert Mills, 11

Cupboard Love

My pet is a dog, her name is Judy. Her favourite trick is, when we are all drinking tea, she thinks she has to have a drink too. She tips the water out of her dish, all over the floor. She then picks up her dish and takes it to dad, who then puts some tea in it for her, while mum is mopping up the flooded kitchen. She then starts barking for some water to be put back into her dish.

Jane Cook 12

When Stanley wants some food he goes into the kitchen and lies on his back and he won't move until something is put down for him.

David Evans, 11

My dog is a good smeller, he can smell my mother cooking about a mile away.

Joy Millett, 9

One rattle of the biscuit tin and you'v got friends for life! They sit and stare with solum eyes, and if you dont take the hint, you get barked at.

Janine Chubb

FOOD

Michael Reynolds, 8

The ways of a dog

Bolt has great character; he runs around the house, most of the day, barking at Mum's hoover and brushes. He whines to go outside and then, a few seconds later, he is wanting to be in again. We got him when he was six weeks, and he was soon up to mischief, tearing the wallpaper, chewing books, letters and magazines, and stealing our food. He managed to eat thirteen lemon cakes in about three seconds. When he has done something wrong he puts his tail between his legs and waggles his ears.
He is also a great rabbit-hunter although he hasn't caught any. He loves watching other dogs on television and was very interested in the Hound of the Baskervilles. He cocked his head from side to side and started to whine as the creature showed it's teeth.

Paul Heselton, 13

Candey is a lady but she douse wees on the lorn shes not very lady like is she by Jessica Barrington.

Jessica Barrington, 6

When ever there is a dog Dougal goes after it but he come back when he has had enoff.

Sara Weastell, 8

Whine

Scratch

woof!

Yelp!

Yowl!

WOOF!

Pant!

Richard Harpham, 13

My dog likes to bury bones behind chairs and in corners when nobody is looking. If he can't find a place he brings the bone to me. After I have buried the bone for him he digs it up and walks off. Last night I found a bone hidden underneath my pillow!

Paul Civi, 12

Ubu. He's the kind of dog that when his master comes in runs all over the house knocking down chairs and tables and skidding on the carpets, then my mother walks in and looks at all the mess, while good old Ubu is pretending to be asleep by the fire!

Piers Stuart Bravery, 11

Caroline Anderson, 11

Toby Whatching Television

Naughties

Suddenly, looking like a dirty tramp, Sandy our dog entered. To cries and shouts of dismay, which soon turned to howls of anger, he sat down on the brand new settee. After being shouted at he procceded to hide under a nearby table. This made everybody felt awful, thinking they had affended him. After being told he was a good boy several times, he procceded to dignefidly walk towards the kitchen. Suddenly, cries of 'Oh no!' Everybody ran into the kitchen to find Sandy full to bursting and one small half-eaten cake. My mother exclaimed, 'He's eaten twenty four'.

This time Sandy didn't make any attempt to sulk. He just sat there unable to move.

Graham Martin

The dog is bad very bad and you wont know Where he has gone because he is small and very fast at runny. He makes cat's cry and eats their food, jumps on the rose bushes and spoils the flowers and Jumps up and down on your bed and you get the blam.

Sally Ann McLeen

Just as we were getting near the bath she jumped up and over it and pulled me forward and I stepped into the bath. There was no point in getting changed because I knew I would be getting even wetter. My mum turned on the water for which I was not ready and I ended up with a faceful of water. When I was just about to start again Shep jumped into me and knocked me backwards and I ended up knocking a bucket of water over that had been put there to rinse the dog off. After all the troubles we got her bathed and let her off her lead she rushed down the garden and rolled in the dirt.
I let my mum bath her, I had had enough.

Stephen Price-Hughes, 11

On a few occasions we have gone out and left Wilby behind, to come back and find a whole box of chocolates opened, and small bites out of all the chocolates except for the type with the strawberry filling, which we presume he likes since there are never any of them left!
On another occasion we were walking by a cornfield, when suddenly Wilby rushed into the corn. After about ten minutes of calling him he came back with a pheasant in his mouth, which I suppose makes up for the chocolates.

Sonya Winner, 11

S Rogers, 15

19

Deirdre Clark, 11

Trouble!

Toby is a black labrador. He is very loving and dopey and can open doors which is a nuisance because he can't shut them.

Christine Stone, 12

Jasper tends to go in the garden with his bone and bark to come in and when we get out there he growls because he does not want to come in. Once we took him out and as soon as we got in he wanted to come in again and as soon as he was in he wanted to go out again he carried on 12 times and in 10 minets.

Scott Freeman, 8

Pat was altogether wicked! Pat used to wait for the milkman to deliver the bread and milk. Then he would go to all the doors and steal the bread.
Pat's other trick was to take everybodies washing off their lines. He took all of his treasures into his hide-away which was at the bottom of our garden. When my Mother found the washing she put it in a basket at the front gate. All the people in our road knew where their washing would be!

Jane Miles

My dog takes me for a walk to the park even when I want to go to the shops

Lea, 6

Michael Culley, 10

21

Dog's eye-view

When I go to sleep on my bed my pet human sleeps with me. In the morning I have to wake him up and get him out of bed. I have taught him to get my breakfast. He is quite intelligent for a human and learns tricks quite easily. I then take my human for a walk and let him loose to wander around the park. Often he gets lost and calls for me and I have to find him. When he gets lost I decide to take him home. My human is very patient and obedient and if I do something wrong my pet shouts at me and to stop him I have to pretend to be scared.

Matthew Prosser, 13

Oh no it's 8 o'clock, she'll be down in a minute to take me for a walk, I don't want to go out into the freezing cold.
What gets me is the stupid way she talks to me, 'Come on Tommy up you get don't you want to go for walky walkies then and get your little tootsy wootsys coldy woldy?' Then she drags me out of my warm basket, puts the lead on and has the cheek to boss me about saying 'Sit' or 'Heel' 'Stand' or 'Stay'.

Hilary Friendship, 13

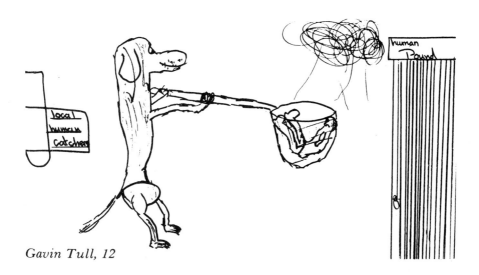

Gavin Tull, 12

Anne Harvey, 13

One very bad dog

I was bored, I just had absolutely nothing to do. My owners had gone wandering off leaving me with a complete stranger they called Gran. This Gran person stooped when she walked, always looking for something she had dropped. Big dogs need a lot of exercise but I didn't get much of that with gran. I trotted out in the garden. I started walking in and out of a large and very muddy puddle, lovely, my feet turned to brown. I was just on my way when my eye was caught by the postman. What a chance, I thought, now I can scare the life out of him, what a weedy looking person. As he came close I could see he was scared of dogs. By the time he got to the gate he had dropped his letters. He opened the gate slowly and said 'Nice doggy, please don't bite me.' He walked carefully up the path sideways, saying 'Nice doggy' all the way. He started back so I barked at him, I've never seen anybody move so fast in all my life, he was out of the gate and up the street in a few seconds. I laughed at him but I was soon bored again. Then what should I see but a fat ginger cat. Brilliant I thought, so creeping up behind him I started barking. Its back arched, his fur stood on end and he spat, then he ran into the house next door. I was really pleased with myself.

The mud had set on my paws so I went back to the puddle. So with nobody else to frighten I decided to mess up Gran's nice polished kitchen floor. I walked twice around the table then around the washing machine. Gran was standing in the doorway looking in dismay at her once spotless floor. When I walked past her she gave me a look 'You naughty dog just look what you've done to my lovely floor'. Then it must have struck her and hands on her head she screamed 'My carpet!'

I wandered out into the garden again and chased the birds. Because it was a sunny day I decided to have a snooze so I lay down and dropped off. While I was sleeping I had a dream, it was a dream I usually have. I'm in the garden sleeping when I suddenly wake up to see a man climbing into the house. Then I woke up. I looked around the garden and I saw what do you think a man in tatty blue overalls climbing through the window. I wasn't sure if it was a dream still. So I kicked myself and it hurt (I couldn't pinch myself because my fingers are the wrong shape). I jumped up and bound up to the window and bit a great big chunck out of the seat of his trousers. He gave a yelp and Gran came racing out of the house. I still had the seats of his pants in my mouth. 'What are you doing'. she screamed, 'let go of the window cleaner immediately.' I didn't know why she was so angry anybody could have made the same mistake. I walked off and went under the tree and sulked for the rest of the day. That's the last time I catch a burgular for her.

Claire Savage

Alan Neish, 9

Postmen beware

Fred is a daffed dog. once We had a new years party And my uncle came with a pare of 20 pound trousers he went home with a pare of 20 pound chewed up to nea hight trousers.

Charles Appleton, 10

I don't like dogs much because if you are a paper boy like me they can be your number one enemy. Other than biting paper boys, milkmen and postmen dogs can be very useful.

Stephen Jupp, 13

My pet is naughty he loves the postman he likes the milkman but he bites my frend most of all.

Fiona Dawson, 10

With snarling jaws my dog awaits the butcher boy with joy.

Andrea Sellers, 10

One night a burglar came to our house and stole some things but Dino was to tired to wake-up So the burglar kept on and on stealing then mummy heard the burglar and woke up daddy and daddy rang the police. So the police-man came and got the burglar and Dino bit the police-mans leg and he wasn't very pleased.

Fiona Lewis, 6

Audrey Pearson

Jamie Heather, 13

Dogs can keep the postman away by chasing him down the path and away with the nasty bills.

Stewart Bressington, 13

Ingrid Sawers, 11

Puppies

My birthday was approaching. Oh how I longed for a dog. I had pleaded with my mum to get me one for five months. I kept on and on nagging, pleading mercilessly, and gradually she seemed to accept the idea, although she hadn't actually said yes.

On my birthday I woke up. My heart began to beat. I got out of bed and rushed down the stairs. I opened our living room door shaking a little. I looked round and then all of a sudden I saw it, a furry, rolled up ball, sleeping silently in a basket. I stopped and stared, hypnotized, and a swoop of love filled my heart. I ran up to it. I longed to pick it up and cuddle it, but I let it sleep. Then suddenly it opened its eyes and gave a loving look at me and yawned. I was so overcome with love, tears stung my eyes. I picked it up and held it against my warm body. Lovingly I stroked it all over. That first day I would never forget, it was one of the happiest days of my life.

Caroline McLoughlin

A Puppy is gay
And allways at play
Thats what puppys are for.
Sarah Round, 10

Alison Lett, 14

29

Hoping for a dog

Dear God, I have a little dog,
He isn't really there,but in the night
When I'm alone I sometimes stroke his hair.
Dear God I love my little dog who isn't really there,
So help him come out from my dreams
And let me keep him in my care.

Sophie Way, 8

If Id got enough money I would buy a spotty dog I would teach
him how to beg for a bone. Id let him sleep on my bed at night
even if Mummy said No.

Paul Skidmore, 7

I wish I could have a pet dog I would call him Boots and he
would be cuddly.
I would take him to the park and his saggy fur would bounce
about I would give him bones to eat and he will be lovable.
But all this can't be true because I am too poor to have a dog.

David Apple, 10

Katie Dickson, 11

How to Persuade Your Parents to Let You Have a Dog

We, that is my sister and I, had wanted a dog for years but it was always Mum who said we couldn't. We nagged and nagged at her until one day she said she would consider it. Of course although she only said she would consider it we started to hunt in the local papers for suitable puppies.

I, and I say that with a certain pride, found an advert for some labrador puppies.

Mum had been helping out with a local jumble sale and was worn out. In fact so worn out that she agreed to go and see the pups. So we all piled into the car including Dad who didn't have much say in the matter.

The puppies were curled up together in a little heap. You couldn't tell which body belonged to which head. We fell in love with them all. Mum did as well. I think?

There was one pup who, when he thought he might get a bit of fuss started romping around and nibbling our feet. We knew then that this was the one for us and even Mum couldn't resist.

Two weeks later we were bringing home a chubby, wobbly ball of fluff.

So for all you dogless children out there here are some does and don'ts when trying to persuade you parents.

Do say that it will guard the house.

Do say it will be a lovely welcome when they come home.

Do say it will keep Mum company during the day.

Do say it won't cost much to feed.

Do say you will train it to be obedient.

Do nag at them.

Do make them go and look at the pups.

Don't tell them it makes puddles on the best lounge carpet.

Don't tell them it might chew things up.

Don't tell them it barks at the neighbours as well as burglars.

Don't tell them it digs up the garden.

Good Luck!

Caroline Ward, 14

31

Welcome!

I open the door and the first thing I meet,
Its a rush of excitement at my feet,
A bundle of happiness jumping with joy.
A short tail wagging like a clockwork toy.
Brown eyes twinkling, ears flapping madly,
Upper lip cocked up, grinning gladly.

Julie Simon, 12

The beautiful little brown and white puppy,
Pink paddy paws, long brown ears,
Every day I arrive home,
Tired and forlorn, and
A little squirming figure greets me,
A lick all over, a paw on my nose,
And then Lucy walks away,
Ready to cheer the next person.

Rachel Peddie, 12

My dog's name is Rudi.
And when I come home from school,
He wags his tail with glee.
When he licks you it's awful,
It's like having a bath,
His tongue is very wet,
And so are you after that.

Fiona McLeod, 9

A dog is always there to greet you.

Tony Beckett, 10

Lee Lucraft, 6

We go to school at nine pm
We have our break and start again
Outside the doors is my furry friend
Waiting in the pourch for the school to end.

Andrea Fyles

School has ended at half past three,
Now I think of my dog waiting for me,
Boss of the Ave, sitting with head up high.
I often wonder why?

There am I, walking down the street, my eyes catch
    sight of my dog.
I STOP!
HE STOPS! and looks at me
I walk nearer to him and he walks nearer to me.
Then when I'm really close to him he runs and
    jumps up at me licking my face.
He never stops barking until we reach our house.

Jacqueline Saneh, 13

No need for words

I love my pet beacouse it is the closes thing I have. And most of all I can talk to it without it talking back to me. You can curse it and it won't say anything back, but it may give you the soft look. And also it is always there when you want it.

Kevin Jones, 14

Its funny my puppy knows just how I feel,
When I'm grumpy he's lumpy and sits by my heel,
When I'm happy he's yappy and squirms like an eel,
Its funny my puppy knows just how I feel.

Lorraine Harvey, 10

When my dog is naughty and I am just about to hit him he lies on his back before I can hit him and pleads with me and makes me rub his tummy, when I have done this I forget about hitting him and he gets up and licks me.

Joy Millett, 9

When a dog has been naugty is crawls and turns over on it's back and puts it's paws on it's tummy.

Kirsty, 8

Lara Mills

Jeanette Holmes, 12

Karen Greensleaves, 11

He cant talk or anser me back. But when he wants something he gives me a sertain look in his eyes or move his body in a sertain way.

Edwina Williams

When you tell her off she will turn her head away or give me her paw, she will lick me so that I will feel sorry for her or she will walk away sit in her bed and sulk.

Karen Williams, 12

Our Wooley Wooter (alias Blue dog) is a medium sized, thickly fur covered and fur brained dog.
Whenever he does anything wrong he always hides in a dark place and all you can see of him are his eyes.

David Cotson, 12

Trixi use to be my constant companion. She looked after me. And when I was sad, she would come and sit at the bottom of the stairs with me, and in her doggy like way, cry.

Sally Keeble, 12

Kuky sniffs at the new person, and
if she likes the person she will sit down
and give the person her paw to shake.

Jacqueline Osei-Tutu

Joyce Larwood, 10

Kerry Thompson, 8

Four-legged friends

A dog is an animal with a wet nose.Which wake you up and gives you lots of love when your friends turn against you.

Clive Scarlett, 10

I like my dog because his name is Turgie And when I go to school he is all sad becawse he does like me and I like him.

Tim Tight, 6

I cudle him and cudle him. He is a dog and his name is Boot. But I call him bodiens and Bootsy-botsy. And he is almost coverd with Black and Whit hairs. I love my dog he makes lots of hairs around the house. But I wood not swop him for a miloin pounds.

Andrew Micferson, 7

If you are lost on a mountain buried in snow, with your lungs fit to burst, the most pleasing sight in the world is that of a big shaggy St Bernard face peering at you, and giving you a friendly lick with a long wet tongue, as if to way 'Well old man here I am!'

Charlotte Keats, 14

Pets are animals you love.
Pets are cuddly but mischievous.
Some people say 'I own a dog'
But deep inside, they don't own it — at all.
But love it and it will love them.

Gareth Callan, 11

He is always freindly and full of fun and I feel safe when he's around.

Jennifer Scard

I've never been able to see
The flowers or the trees
I live in the dark
I never see children playing in the park
But there is something no-one can hear smell or see
And that's the special bond between my dog and me
Even my blindness can't smother
The love we have for one another
If for one minute my eyes would mend
So I could see my lifelong friend.

Alice Whelan, 10

He's strong and powerfull clever and wise sometimes naughty and sometimes kind. And im so glad that he's all mine.

Jennifer Scard, 11

Zoe Clarke, 10

Old faithful

My dog is called Jason and he is about 56. He is rather podgy.
He sometimes likes to lick my face which I hate! He has a long
pink tounge that sticks out of his mouth because it is so long.
He is very tame and hardly ever bites as he only owns four
teeth.

Andrea Nelson, 10

Shandy used to be a naughty little pup,
Chasing me all around the place,
But I loved her.

Shandy was very wild,
And very dirty,
But I loved her.

But now she is only a lazy bundle of fur.
But I still love her.

Suzanne Francis, 10

His slopy rugged tongue like a scrubing brush, His eyes like chocolate, He breaths the air of lonlyness And crys the tears of love.

Julie Martin

Nicola Sinclair, 8

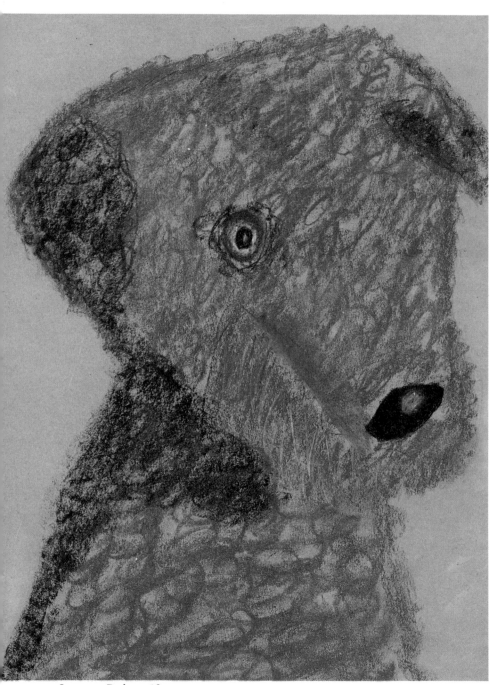

Joanna Baker, 12

Two old friends

She bought him ten years ago. He's old now, but she still loves him. He's her only companion. Everyone else has left her, but he'll not go. He's the one who comforts her when the full misery of her life hails upon her.

They live for each other. When one is ill the other tends with caring, loving attention. They have the same feelings, same likes and dislikes. Everything is shared.

Yet one is a dog, and the other an old, frail lady.

Simon Perkins, 12

Sitting by the fire's harth in an old arm chair. Watching the flickers of red, orange, green and blue flames dancing in the fire. His eyes sad and tired, grey as a seagull's wing, but friendly and kind. He is unloved by the outside world but within his home he has all the love in the world. His withered hand rests upon the warm neck of his old friend, patting him slowly and smileing with love and effection.

The old man's eyes twinkle as his life long friend licks his hand lovingly. Nothing in the world could part them, for all they need is each other and between them lies happyness.

Sonya Dorraine Haynes

The old man stumbled on his weary legs.
Behind him a terrier followed obediently.
Everyday, every depressing day, the man and dog made
    that journey to the door.
The man saw no one, except a blind neighbour who came
    round to give him meals.
The two old creatures, terrier and social outcast would eat.
Both were old and frail.
Both lived for each other.
Both were neglected by nearly everything and everyone.
Both knew they must die . . .
Sometime.

Sarah Chinn, 10

Remembering

A shaggy brown shape rests on the table:
Still quite still.
Its eyes are closed, its body is cold, its golden tail
Flops over the side.
What is it? When did it happen? What does it all mean?
'Bout noon ma'am. On Teapenny Hill. A man in a van.
A gruff voice jerks from behind.
Focus anew on the figure;
A dark trickle glows from its side —
Suddenly light dawns.
Stow the basket away, hang up the collar,
Forget about the mud on the kitchen floor,
Throw the mutton bone into the waste.
Shut your ears to the playful bark;
Blind your eyes to the friendly face,
For all have vanished.
You are desolate, your life is bare.
A shaggy brown shape rests on the table.
Dead, quite dead.
I am bereft of Bronze.

M Cotthorpe, 17

I remember the way she would
   chase the seagulls along the golden sands
And rub her wet nose against your leg
   when it was dinner-time.
Then one day she was no longer there.
No more the wet, shiny nose
   and the big brown eyes
That stared at you from an infathomable deepness
She was with us no more
But her memory will never fade
Till the day I die.

Sara Scamell, 15

Lucas was born before I was, so when I came along he was 'just there'. He grew up with me and I looked upon him as a brother and a human, never a dog. It was natural seeing him around; Lucas was an important part of my life. During our time together, I got two sisters, both of which adored Lucas.
Ten years later, my dog had lost his gleaming coat, but under the tired and ill appearance he was the same dog. One winter's day, just after his twelfth birthday, we were playing Ludo in the sitting room when Mummy came in, she said, 'Daddy's got something to tell you.' We went into the kitchen and there was Dad with a golden labrador at his feet. 'Where's Lucas?' we asked. And Dad burst into tears.

Nicola Goldstone, 12

Bonnie with your sad brown eyes
Don't look that way, don't let it be me you despise
You've lived with us for seven long years
And I'll remember you still, through all of my tears.

I wish I could leave and go with you,
But it can't be that way and you know that is true
You are more than a dog, a little pet
You're my only friend, and now here comes the vet.

Don't cry now Bonnie, be good be strong
Go with this man and he'll do you no wrong
I'll say goodbye as I stroke your soft head
Bonnie with your sad brown eyes,
Please don't look that way.

Annette Hartley, 15

For glorious hours we've sat — a pair,
My favourite pet — and me.
To me he's always been special,
In my heart, he never did die.

Carole Howlett, 13

Other funny furries

Flossy my pet hamster is fantasicly friendly, and has only bit me twice.

Victoria Lawrie, 10

Playing with pets e.g. rabbits, dogs is different from playing with humans. You feel more superior.

Arati Shah, 12

Rachel Llewellyn, 9

I would like to have a mouse. Just think if mice were like dogs, we would have to take our mice for walks and the cans of food would be so small that you could be 30 and you would still not of spent over £2 And just think of the size of the kennel to put them in, I bet when you are nailing the bits together you'd bang your thumb.

Siobhan Carron, 9

There was a film called Jaws, it was very famous. I would make a film called Gums a shark worse than its bite. Of course it would have its own set of false teeth, and a denture repair kit. Gums will also do stunts like eating fish and chips without his teeth falling out. Gums has his own Rolls Royce and surfboard. I can tell this film is going to be fantastic.

Andrew Scattergood

I was going to do my animal lovers badge and I was using Herbert through out the badge. I had to take Herbert to Brownies. It was just on that day when Herbert died. I was very unhappy. Only I did my craft badge instead.

Emma Critchley

A tortoise is like London trains, running late.

Neil Lawrence, 12

Tijen Hassan, 6

Pets galore!

A pony is something which you blow all your pocket money on, to buy a new bridle, then it breaks into the tack room and chews it to bits.

A pony is something which you feed and exercise faithfully, cosset and love, and then goes lame the day before the show.

A pony is something which wins the junior jumping at Windsor and then bites the Queen.

A pony is something I wouldn't be without.

Jackie Lynch, 14

B Downie, 7

I Wished I had a horse
One day he stopped Suddenly
and I flew int o s pace
Now I dont Wish I had one

William Cohen, 7

A Pet comes in the morning and wacks you for his breakfast and you can chase her roned The garden And i can chace him round The Bened too

Dionne Neysmith, 7

A pet is a ball of play
A pet is a ball of Mischieve
A pet is a bundle of trouble.
Rohan Whittle

One day a boy called Mark put his fingers in the cage and said, 'Who's a pretty boy then?' Ginger bit Mark and he had to go to hospital.
Michelle Harrison, 10

I love my pet because he doesn't scratch me he scratches my brother.
Lee McAlpine, 10

Simon Massey, 6

Imaginary thingies

I would like to own a dragon so that it would sit outside my door and stop my wee sister from coming into my room at six o'clock.

Alison Campbell, 9

One night I dreamt of owning a croacacat. Croacacats are half croacadile and half cat. Dogs are afraid of croacacats. Because when they see the cat part of a croacacat they jump at that part. Then the croacacat either walks away or turns and frigtens the dog back to its basket. Croacacats are quite funny about having a wash or a bath they lie on the edge of the shore whith the croacadile part in the water and the cat part not in the water.

Steven Deller, 8

Michael Tusch, 8

In front of me was a small box with my initials on it. Inside was a worm-like thing. It had six legs and was striped with bright colours and had a lable round it's neck: 'You Harriet Kevans have been chosen out of all carth-beings to look after ZITTON 7 until he is old enough to return to the planet Butlins.'

Harriet Kevans, 12

If you ever come to our house,
Keep your parents out of sight,
Or my sister's little monster,
Will devour them in one bite!

My sister's little monster,
Ate my aunty for its tea,
And my uncle for its dinner,
But it couldn't catch me!

My sister's little monster,
Lives among the raspberry canes,
I don't know what it is,
But I avoid it just the same!

Carolyn Gardner, 13

Sarah Palmer, 7

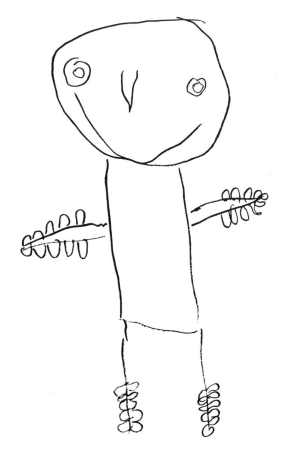

I would not like
king kong for a
pet beconce he
would strongle you.

Darren Ward, 5

More thingies

My dream of owning an unusual pet, would be a panther. No ordinary panther, but a huge black panther, with saucer-like green eyes. She would be fed on eight cans of cat meat a day, and one or two of my enemies. She would scare my big brother out of his wits.

Yasmin Amir, 12

I wish I could have an animal like this discriptoin two legs of a Cat, two legs of an Elephant, half a body of a Liazrd, half of a dog's body, a Snakes tail, bats ears, frogs eyes, a bulb Tongue, a Rat's nose. I would like a pond of paraner fish and a rattle Snake pit. That's what. I would have only one of the animals of course I don't want to over do it.

Alan Wright, 10

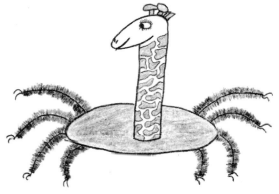

I would like a spiraffe.

A spiraffe is a cross between a tarantula spider, and a tiny giraffe. I suppose it could have been called soemthing else, but a girder sounds silly.
If I ever got a spiraffe, I would keep it in my Mum's greenhouse. I would take it for walks around deserted parks because otherwise I would feel silly walking about with a spiraffe on a lead.

Timothy Atkinson, 13

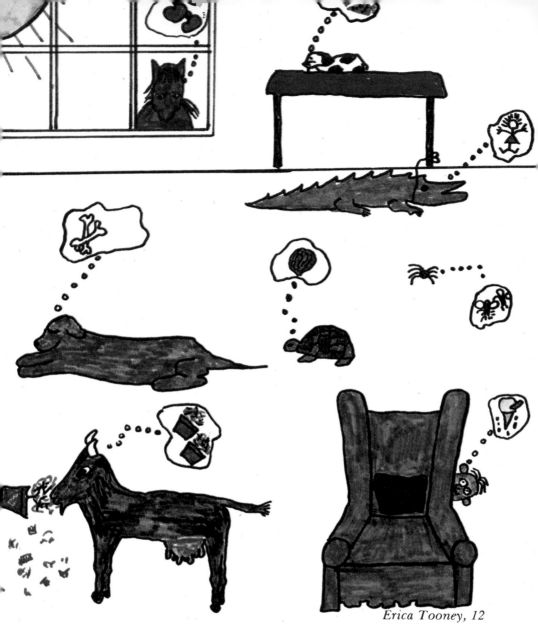

Erica Tooney, 12

A pet is a waste disposal unit ready and waiting.

Jayne Burwell

Greedy gobblies

Susie is my tortoise and a very fine animal she is, when we went to collect her from her previous owner the lawn was covered with little tunnels so we knew we had a little Terror on our hands.

Susie will eat anthing and I really mean anything, chicken, eggs, beef, dead slugs, slug killer, snails, cheese, ice cream, spaghetti, she will eat anything you give to her.

Her speciality is jumping off walls any shape or size, actually I think she's mad.

Frances Morton

In Summer Alice, our tortoise, has her usual escapes. She explores six gardens in about 2 hours then people find her eating there prize lettuces. They know who to give it to. Us. Fortunatly she sleeps half the year.

Catherine Sugrue, 11

I'm the lucky owner of two flower-eating tortoises. We used to have a pretty garden, but now all we have is a tangled mass of stems. One fortunate thing is that I don't have to cut the grass.

Paul Turner, 12

My name is Chino. The only things I will eat are steak, beef, lamb, potato, turkey, eggs and a few little extras. Oh yes! and I like one level spoonful of gravy on the top.

Lucie Prateley, 11

Alice Bird, 11

Loving

When I come home from school I call out 'Hello Susy, hello Lucy', and they Baa 'Hello Katie'. My dog comes bounding up with a lick at the front and a wag at the back. His longing eyes look up at me and he pleads with me to come and play. Soon there is a soft feeling around my legs and my cat comes purring her greeting. I would never like to be without my pets. They play with me when I am glad, they comfort me when I am sad, I love my pets.

Kate Counsell, 13

The first word I ever said was 'Mot'. I used to talk to him in my own language and he used to pretend that he could answer me in his own way.

Sian Jones, 14

I love my budgeriguard.

Lyn Evans

Pets are for loving
Care for your pets.

Emma Crouch, 10

A pet is someone to share sad thoughts.

Claire Holiday, 11

I love my pet because she never lets me down
When I am sad she comforts me
When I am ill she stays by me
If I am lonely I think of her and
   everything seems bright
She is always ready to listen, contentedly
Lying there her brown eyes blinking
Her warm body curled up next to the fire
If I am worried I tell her and she seems to say
It will be alright.

Samantha Jane Richardson, 11

Old people like to care for someone but find it hard with people.

Pat Evans, 14

Pets are lovely things to have. All generations are fond of them. When you are little, you have a pet as a playmate. It sleeps on your bed.
When you get older, you still care but you don't show it as much. If you have a budgie or hamster, instead of cooing at the cage you talk to it and comment on how tired you are. Some people have quite a good conversation with their budgies.
Then when you are old and living alone, a pet becomes one of the most important things in your life. It is your only real companion, who will sit by you or snuggle up on your lap. The only being who says in his own mysterious way that he loves you.

Audrey Ann Wolffs, 14

Soft and warm

Why I love my pet because they are fluffz and cuddley when they howl they look so up set you could almost cry and when you see there eyes watering you fell relly upset when you here them sneeze you fell you want to give them a hankey chefe when you see there tail waggling you want to stroke it.

Mark Horton

I got my horse on the Friday night,
I thought he was a beautiful sight.
I holded him in a warm embrass,
As he tuch my heart
With his gently face.

Alison Dowling

I love ponies and horses because they have soft muzzles (velverty kind of nose) and they blow into your hair, which is a lovely feeling.

Selina Westcott, 10

I do not really know why people keep pets but I do no why I keep pets, the reason is that I think they are warm and cuddly.

Judith Turner, 8

My pet is my own little baby some~ thing small and cuddle warming.

Andrew George, 10   *Edwina Williams, 13*

Claire Taylor, 10 ▷

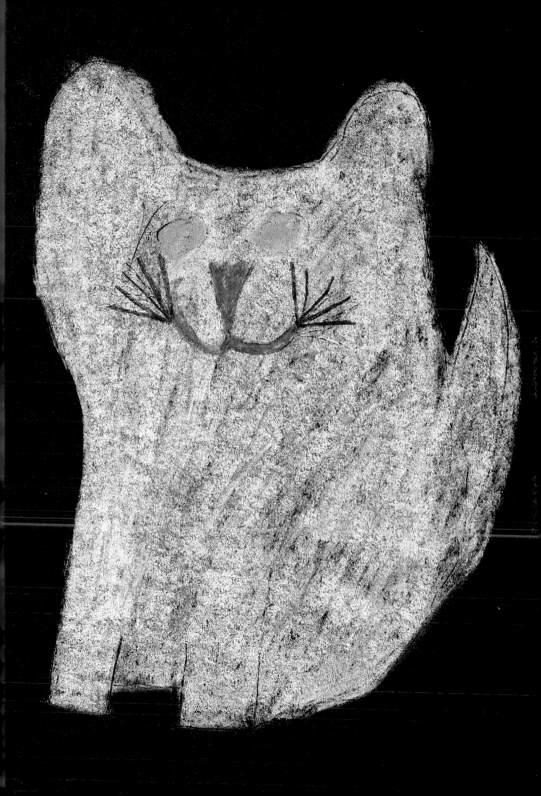

Children against cruelty

The doctors would not like it if a big hairy ape came along and gave them drugs and killed them off one by one. Science fiction films are just as bad because only a few weeks ago in a film called the Andromidar Strain they killed off animals just for a film.

Andrew Coxall, 9

I mean how would you like to be probed and dissected, or every time you come out of your house you get shot at by someone? Why not just leave wild animals alone just like they leave you alone?

J C Wakeford, 13

I think there are too many pets in this country. Look at all the poor little dogs and cats who are thrown out of cars and left in a wood. Nobody cares in the least. Then there are all the dogs in the kennels, some being put down every day. It's very cruel but no-one wants them. My main advice is, don't give people pets as presents unless they really want them and won't get tired of them after three or four months.

Robert Jack, 11

A dog is a mans best friend everyone says, I wonder why there are so many strays.

Michael Medlock, 12

His name is Shaggy the dog

We found him shaking with fear
We called him Shaggy because of his fur
But why was he alone without an owner?
I wonder why?

He was sitting there with big brown eyes
He was scared of passers-by
Oh why didn't anyone care?
I wonder why?

He's much better now with us
I'll not forget finding him.
I'll always cuddle and care for him
But I can't get over anyone leaving him
I still wonder why.

Amanda Blair, 12

Sarah Chinn, 10

Flying free

Bounding, beautifull and brown,
Long legs and big, blue eyes,
Mane flapping in the wind,
Strides forming the rythm of music,
A horse, so beautifull,
Gliding along in the air.

Audrey Ann Wolffs, 14

A run to the park
A swim in the lake
Three rabbits to chase
A run home in haste

Master is coming
All of us hurrying
No time to wait
A dog's life is great!

Heather Drummond, 13

Winter keeps you in my home, but when summer comes you
fly free all alone. To think we once owned you, to think you
were ours; and now you are away from us many, many miles.
Nature has come between us and nature desires that you stay in
your world and we stay in ours. But the wind won't stop
blowing, and from the sun we still get light, like our
friendship is still growing in our bodies deep inside.

Louise Schachter, 9

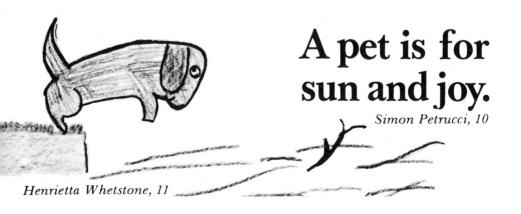

A pet is for sun and joy.

Simon Petrucci, 10

Henrietta Whetstone, 11

Together we have fun
   playing in the park
Under the summer sun
   where my dog began to bark.

Playing on the swings
   we had a smashing time
Suddenly we thought we had wings
   all through the summer time.

Kevin Thomas, 13

Nicola Coley, 7

Thank you Beth

To lose your parents must be the worst thing that can happen to anyone. One minute they are there, the next minute they are gone and there is nothing you can do about it but cry. When my parents died in a car crash I just did not want to go on living and I would never have made it if Beth had not entered my life.

I was to live with my Aunt Ellen who lived in Cornwall. I had never met her before but my mother had often said that she was kind and generous.

Thinking of my mother brought tears to my eyes but I brushed them away as the train I was travelling on came screeching to a halt.

With eyes still blurred with tears I saw a tiny country station. One low-roofed building and a sign saying Jakeley told me I had arrived at my new home. A worried looking woman hurried onto the platform. In one hand she clutched a large grey purse, in the other a long dog lead and fixed to the end was Beth. I quickly got out of my carriage and looked at the woman. She came towards me tugging at the leash.

'You must be Ann . . . how are you dear?,' The woman looked at me, she was about fifty, with grey hair and brown eyes. She smiled at me calmly but I thought she looked flustered and had probably only just received the letter telling of my parents death and my arrival.

'Hello . . . er . . . Aunt Ellen . . . yes I'm Ann and I'm quite well thank you.' 'Good,' she said absentmindedly; she paused then rushed on 'This dog here she's . . . er . . . a present for you . . . her name's Beth.'

Beth, I thought . . . Beth . . . my dog. Then I looked from the dog to my aunt and said, 'Oh, Aunt Ellen she's lovely but you shouldn't have.'

'Well she didn't cost much and besides you need a friend. It's the summer holidays and I'm always so busy . . .'

'Oh, well thank you, yes thank you very much.'

We were silent all the way home and most of the time through tea and an inspection of my room and the house. Only when I was getting ready for bed did I speak to Beth, 'Thank you Beth ... thank you for coming to me ... I know you can help.'

During the following summer my aunt spent little time with me so I went to the beach to swim and took long walks over the fields and nearby woods. I went walking for miles and Beth was always there, like my shadow. Following the same paths I took, stopping with me to listen to some bird or watch a wild animal scurry to its home, always there where she was needed most. If I stopped sometimes to think of my parents and let the tears trickle down my cheek she would jump onto my lap and lick them away then bark and leap, showing off, distracting me, making me forget the death of my parents. Beth was the best pet anyone could have. The summer was long and hot. At times I despaired at life but Beth was there. She helped me make friends, meet new people, find things to do and places to go. Beth helped me break down the barrier I had formed with the world after my parent's death. She helped me rebuild my life. Beth was a dog in a million.

A Osborn

Robert Glover, 12

Some other interesting EXLEY titles now available

See Britain at Work, £4.95
This guidebook details hundreds of glassworks, craft workshops, potteries, factories etc. open to the public and to schools. An invaluable family reference book.

Shopping by Post, £5.50
Hundreds of firms which will supply goods by post. 'An excellent book' (Marge Proops).'Extraordinarily comprehensive' (Sheila Black). Invaluable for those who live far from good shops.

The Magic of London's Museums, £4.95
This illustrated guide to all London's museums — almost 100 of them — will provide endless ideas for a rainy day. Ideal for teachers, parents and holidaymakers.

Dear World, £6.95
'How I would put the world right, by children of 50 nations'. An unusual and beautifully illustrated book, in colour.

What is a husband? £2.50
7,500 real wives answered that question and the best quotes are here. Pithy, beautiful, rude, hilarious, sad, romantic. Buy a copy for your anniversary!

Old is great: £2.50
A book that pokes fun at youth and revels in the first grey hairs of middle age. 'An irreverent sometimes bawdy, loo-side book for anyone over 30. Furiously funny', says the Good Book Guide.

Grandmas & Grandpas, £2.50
'A Grandma is old on the outside and young on the inside.' This charming little book with all the entries written by grandchildren solves many a present problem.

To Dad, £2.50
'Fathers are always right, and even if they're not right, they're never actually wrong.' Dads will love this book. Also in the series: *To Mum, Happy Families, CATS (and other crazy cuddlies), DOGS (and other funny furries)*.

All these books are obtainable through your local bookshop, or by post from Exley Publications, 63 Kingsfield Road, Watford, Herts, WD1 4PP. Please add 10p in the £ as a contribution to postage.